I AM WHO GOD SAYS I AM

LIVING MY LIFE ON PURPOSE
I AM WHO GOD SAYS I AM.
LIVING MY LIFE ON PURPOSE.

Copyright © 2019 Kiesha L Peterson

All rights reserved. No part of this publication may be reproduced, distributed, or transmitted in any form or by any means, including photocopying, recording, or other electronic or mechanical methods, without the prior written permission of the publisher, except in the case of brief quotations embodied in critical reviews and certain other noncommercial uses permitted by copyright law. For permission requests, email the compiler, addressed "Attention: Permissions Coordinator," at the address below:

ISBN- 978-1-7338696-3-8

Library of Congress: 2019914160

LIVING MY LIFE ON PURPOSE

THE DEDICATION

MY CHILDREN AND GRANDCHLDREN;

E. Isaiah Davis (Trinity Nicole, Alexis Annette, Ayden Isaiah)

Ahja Dominique Smith (Alijah Malik Barns)
Toby Sierra Peterson (Sakhar Tyreese)

To YOU, I leave my Legacy.

THE FOREWORD

In a world where people ask themselves, *"What's my purpose?"* followed by, *"Why am I here?"*, my theory is that those who ask such are those who lack some of life's most challenging experience. Challenge permits one to gain experience. Experience provides wisdom and wisdom, knowledge. Knowledge gives the assurance one needs in order to truly understand his or her self-worth. It also gives one the confidence and grants clearance to side with making decisions that align with what confirms direction and ultimately, one's destination. Books like this help to give clarity, creativity and confirmation to those who ask the questions *and* desire the answers. The collaborative of these authors expressing their life experiences, mixed with wisdom and a touch of knowledge, will cause these questions to become inspiration that makes one a movement and not a monument.

Knowing and understanding one's purpose is two different things. As we develop, we can determine the difference between the two. Understanding is an essential part of one making his or her mark in the world. Knowing one's strengths and certainly weaknesses, is a clear indication of maturity. Maturity plays a huge part in a person's ability to handle all that comes with the territory of understanding. It amazes me that so many folks want to move into purpose while simultaneously asking for directions to get there. The bible helps us to understand that it's God who will direct my path, order my steps and lead me to righteousness for His name sake. But there are some things I must do in order to assure that my steps are not wasted. I must TRUST Him. I must believe He is who I know Him to be and allow Him to be so. I must WAIT on Him. I have to believe His time is the best and only time and when it's time, I will be ready because He'll make sure of it.

Lastly, we must be WILLING TO WORK until opportunity presents itself. It's been said that if you stay ready, when the time comes, you won't have to get ready. I truly believe, for those of us who've been trusting, waiting and willing to work will receive the manifestation of the promise that's connected to purpose. Endure the process and the pain that comes with it, trying to stop us from reaching for the finish line with victory on our mind. It's very important for us to understand that without a commitment you will never start, but more importantly, without consistency, you'll never finish. God has promised purpose to those who are willing to endure the pain that is attached without any complaints. Are you ready to go after what God has for you? Are you ready to accept what God allows? No time to quit, quitting is not an option. Don't quit; just finish. The bible gives us these words: *The race is not given to the swift nor the battle to the strong but to he that endures to the end.* All you have to do is hang on in there. Remember, the best part about the journey is not arriving at the end; it's about enjoying how you made it so far.

Bishop Eric Wright, Sr.
Assistant Pastor of The Empowering Believers Church and
Vice Presiding Prelate of the Empowering Believers Apostolic International Network

THE PREFACE

I began writing at an early age. As a teen I wrote songs, comic books, poetry and short stories. Like most teens, I had no idea I would be where I am today. Growing up, I always wanted to be a high school Math Teacher; I never imagined I would be a four-time Self-Published Author, an Amazon Best-Selling and International Best-Selling Author and a Compiler.

In walking this path, there have been numerous times where I had to remind myself to stop second guessing what God has already ordained. There are two co-authors who have been here since conception, but many have come and gone. Several who seemed excited to be a part of the project kind of fell off by the wayside of the road. It seemed as though I was losing co-authors each week until finally, God formed this awesome group of sixteen co-authors who said yes.

I woke up one morning with determination in my heart. I had to remind myself that God would not give me something as valuable as this just to take it back. Although this is my first Anthology, I am now convinced that God had to weed out those who were not really in it for the right reasons. Their lack of desire to participate turned out ok. God was just making room for those who were ready, willing and had the desire to fulfill what *He* had in store for this book.

Even though I have a solo book titled, *I Am Who God Says I Am,* God gave me a similar yet different vision for this book. *I Am Who God Says I Am: Living My Life On Purpose* was given to me one Sunday morning as I was teaching my first Sunday School class at The House of Kingdom Revolution (Pastor Daryl C. Beecham II).

This book has been designed to encourage, motivate and draw you, our readers, not just to a better life, but to what precedes a better life - a better relationship with God.

THE ACKNOWLEDGEMENTS

Rachel Louise "Lou" Johnson – You are the BEST! You have never made me feel like a stepchild. You are truly a Mother By Nature. Thank you for your unconditional love and support.

Aunt Gerald, Aunt Liz, Aunt Mary & Aunt Pat – Thank you for being the loving and nurturing women I needed to see me safely through this journey called LIFE. I know G.P. would appreciate it.

Bishop Claude L. & Mother Dessie M. Campbell – Thank you for planting the seed and laying the foundation to the path of my God Ordained ministry, The Absolute Word Ministries.

Dr. Marilyn E. Porter – I would have to write a book in order to tell the world of how grateful I am for you being the woman God has called you to be. Through Him, you have obliterated the box that I tried so hard to hide in. I will continue to walk the line of ABSOLUTE.

Minister Michelle "Mamma Chelle" Flagg – I Thank God for allowing our paths to cross. Thank you so much for taking me under your wings. Thank you soo much for your "YES" to be my Editor. I Love You Soooooo Much! You may not have given birth to me, but you will forever be my Mamma Chelle.

Ms. Kocysha LaShaun – Thank You! Thank You! Thank you soo much for your help and your support. You didn't hesitate when I asked you to be Co-Editor. I Love You! And may God Continue to Bless you on your endeavors.

Mother Marion "Sgt. Mother" Thompson – Words cannot express how much I appreciate your love, your support and your stern discipline.

Juanita E. Gaynor – Girl, where do I begin? I thank God for your 'Yes', from the YV Daily Devotional Group to wherever God leads us, you have enhanced the true meaning of "Sisterhood." I Love You to infinity and beyond (in my Buzz Lightyear's voice).

THE INTRODUCTION

I thought *I Am Who God Says I Am: Living My Life On Purpose* started on August 30, 2018, the first day I contacted Dr. Porter about compiling an anthology. Then I realized, it started on Friday, September 26, 1969, the day I was born. That day, I was born into my destiny.

The stories in this book will cover various ups and downs, ins and outs and things in life that would make many want to throw in the towel. I know the words that cover the pages of this book will not only touch your MIND, your HEART and your SOUL, they will also ENCOURAGE and EMPOWER YOU to Live Your Life On Purpose.

This book was written to help those who are having a difficult time playing the hand life has dealt them. We all have been through some rough times. Some of us are still there. But we have learned by putting it all in God's hands, there is nothing we cannot accomplish.

I AM WHO GOD SAYS I AM

TABLE OF CONTENTS

Dedication vi

Foreword vii

Preface viii

Acknowledgements xiv

Introduction xvii

   1. Carol Craven 25

      I AM Favored by God

   2. Deana Williams 39

      I AM Enough

   3. Debra Davis 55

      I AM Evolving

   4. Jennifer Nsenkyire 69

      I AM Fearless

   5. Juanita E. Gaynor 87

      I AM Restored

6. Kocysha LaShaun 101

I AM Chosen

7. Michelle Flagg 117

I AM Found

8. Montell McClain 131

I AM Resilient

9. Sharifa Stirgus 145

I AM An Overcomer

10. Kiesha L. Peterson 161

I AM Who God Says I Am

First Supporter Mentions 180

In Memoriam 187

LIVING MY LIFE ON PURPOSE

Dear Friend,

Our mission is to inspire you to purpose! Please pay attention to the space provided for you at the end of each chapter; where you can create your own "I AM …" affirmation.

The Authors

I AM ...

Favored

Enough

Evolving

Fearless

Restored

Chosen

Found

Resilient

An Overcomer

I am who GOD says I AM.

Carol Danielle Craven is the third and youngest daughter of Colen and Bertha Craven. Originally from North Carolina, relocation to New Carrolton, Maryland proved to be pivotal to her career. During her three years stay there, Carol became a published author. She also became a small business owner of Southern Comfort by Carol, a Southern-style cuisine catering service. She is the mother of four, grandmother of two and looking forward to the addition of another grandchild in the Fall. Carol is also an alumnus of the illustrious Shaw University and holds a B.A. in Religion and Philosophy. She cherishes her family, children and entrepreneur activities. She treasures her relationship with God and her theological community involvements.

I AM WHO GOD SAYS I AM

E-mail

caroldaniellecraven@yahoo.com

Website

https://www.southerncomfortbycarol.org

Phone

336-965-9470

CAROL'S DEDICATION

I would like to dedicate this book to my parents, children and grandchildren. Their ideas, wisdom and energy allowed me to persevere.

CAROL

I AM Favored by God

"God surrounds me with His favor."
Psalm 5:12

When I was younger, I honestly believed that what we perceived as "luck" was Really favor from God. When something good happened, I thought it was a combination of the universe and God giving us something pleasurable in return for something good we had done. As I have matured and gained wisdom, I now understand that favor is a measure of grace from the Lord. Favor is His countenance on our faces. Favor is His divine protection, mercy and love for His creation. Favor is His sweet way of giving us the desire of our hearts.

February 2017 began the journey of a health crisis for me. Ultimately, it would teach me patience and the power of God's amazing grace. It was during that season where I would learn the power of His might to intentionally magnify my praise for all He had done in my life. I grew exponentially in faith, confidently in His blessed assurance and in a formidable ability to totally trust Him at His word. Everything I needed and wanted would be found in the courage I would use in my healing process. For three nonconsecutive months, I endured three falls. One occurred in February, one in April and another in June. The fall in June would send me to the hospital. That particular fall was very different from the others. My teenage son and one of my daughters came in from school to find me passed out on the floor. When I came to, I could not tell them how I fell or how long I possibly had been on the floor prior to them arriving home from school. From that defining moment, to a diagnosis in August seemed as though it were an eternity. Several tests were taken and reviewed. Arthritis settled in my feet. My hands began to swell. In addition, no medication I took for pain would remedy what my body was feeling. It was a scary time for me. I was in

Maryland, five hours away from my family in North Carolina. Aside from my work family, I only had one other friend. Ironically at that point in time, she had accepted a job out of state.

    During those months, I cried, prayed and attempted to bargain with God. I did not want to return to North Carolina. I had left there in 2015 because my life needed a change. I was unhappy in my career and marriage. My spiritual tank had hit empty. I partially felt I was running away, yet I had the unction to begin a new chapter that would definitely bring favor to my life. I did not know how blessed I would become by saying yes to God at a time in my life that was so uncertain. There was major friction, stress and sadness. Everything I thought I stood for felt mismanaged and incongruent. I began to feel a loss of strength and integrity. All I had was my faith in God, yet even in the midst of feelings of unworthiness, I still managed to hold on to enough faith to trust Him.

As I moved through months of pain, indecision and grief, I continued to persevere although my pain increased, my attendance at work decreased and my ability to drive eventually ceased. With my pain, and attendance issues and the inability to drive, that eventually cost me an amazing position at work. Here I was now unemployed, away from family, depressed and living off of savings I knew would possibly run out before my health improved. By December I knew my return home was inevitable. That added to my sadness. I did not want to feel as though I had failed. There were a few people who said, "She won't make it. She will be back." I ignored the naysayers and stood on trusting God. I prayed. I pushed. I worked. I maintained. I overcame. I survived. I trusted God. I was reminded of His providence over my life. I was reminded I have a saving grace and that I was loved. I was reminded that He was and is the Master of Suddenly! That eight-month period would prove to be a dark place, yet I found God's found favor enveloped my life and illuminated His loving ways. He

provided for me, stretched me and matured me. He brought my family together to care for me during my illness. Got was able to show me the power of His might and allowed me to have a triumphant return.

All I had endured in 2017 did not prepare me for the miracles that happened for me in 2018! Returning home in January of that year was hard. I felt as though some of the sadness I had left behind three years prior was still there, ready to disrupt my peace. I made up my mind to face it and dissolve it. I faced insurmountable obstacles in Maryland, but my life had been nothing short of a miracle. While living there I became a published author. I finished a long-distance study program with UNC Chapel Hill. I became the proud owner and creator of my catering service, Southern Comfort by Carol! God blessed me to use my gifts and talents in order to transition into entrepreneurship. Since returning to North Carolina, I have become ServSafe certified to cook and have contributed to two additional anthologies. I also was able to return to my former nursing agency where I had worked a pleasurable and memorable eight years before I moved to Maryland. I returned to a raise in salary which included the option to create my desired schedule. That allowed me to continue to build and invest in my small business ventures. Once again, God showed the power of His consistency over my life and that of my family. God can do anything but fail.

His mercy over my life has given me the chance to grow in grace and develop an even more powerful relationship with Him. He continues to prove Himself to me daily! Even though I face residual health battles due to nerve damage, I am no longer in need of equipment to move about and my driving restriction has been lifted. God returned me back to my family, a wonderful job and the opportunity to successfully forge ahead in establishing my own business. No one can ever tell me that favor does not exist. No one can tell me that His love does not cover a multitude of mishaps. No one can tell me that He is not faithful and true to His promises. It is God's desire to bless us exceedingly and abundantly. He has restored, renewed and redistributed my faith. My gratefulness is indescribable.

As I bring my chapter to a close, I want to encourage all who reads my message to never give up, to never lose hope and to never believe that his favor will not manifest in your life.

Tests, trials and tribulations will show up in our lives. They will likely usher in uncertainty, be hidden in the unforeseen and present themselves amid tumultuous circumstances seemly impossible to endure. I want to encourage and remind you of three truths. Never give up. God will sustain you through any process. Never lose hope. Expect God, who cannot fail, to be true to His unfailing word. Never believe that God's favor will not manifest in your life. His favor surrounds you like a shield. He's always got you covered. Always.

LIVING MY LIFE ON PURPOSE

My Reflections

I AM _____

_____

_____

_____

_____

_____

_____

_____

_____

_____

_____

_____

_____

_____

_____

_____

_____

_____

_____

_____

_____

I AM WHO GOD SAYS I AM

Deana Williams is the proud Mother of one daughter: Kaitlyn. Deana is a licensed Minister, Amazon best-selling author, Motivational & Inspirational Speaker, Certified Transformational Life Coach, Mentor, Advocate and Contributor for THV11. She is Founder of "Taking My Life Back" Empowerment Conferences and Devine Purpose, LLC. Deana was determined to defy all odds stacked against her; she graduated high school in 1988 and college in 1993 while raising her younger sibling. She has practiced Physical Therapy for over 26 years. She is a member of Delta Sigma Theta, Inc. Deana received her Honorary Doctorate of Divinity. Deana gives God all the glory! Her relationship with God is of utmost importance. Deana values family. Deana strives to use her platform to engage, educate, equip and empower people to heal, forgive and move forward. Deana's goal is to give voice to victims and power to the powerless! Forgiveness heals, love wins!

Email

dwnkt@comcast.net

Website

http://getmoved.org

Phone

501-993-1705

Facebook

https://www.facebook.com/DevinePurposeandAboutFaceLifeCoaching

Instagram

https://www.instagram.com/getmoved

Twitter

https://www.twitter.com/dwnkt

DEANA'S ACKNOWLEDGMENTS

To my family with love & admiration!

Thanks everyone for encouraging me to do greater!

DEANA'S TRIBUTE

*In Honor of
My Late Parents*

James and Delores Williams

DEANA

I AM Enough

Born Blandine Williams, but known by all as Deana, I was raised and reared in the Delta. West Helena, Arkansas was a place where family and community were both of great value. Family established your identity while the community shaped and molded you. I often heard people say, "You are a product of your society". West Helena was rich in heritage, but for some it was an ever-evolving valley of poverty. I was born with certain rites of passage because of who my parents were. My dad was an entrepreneur, an established businessman who was well known to the local and surrounding areas. However, the blessing of having both parents soon became what I felt to be a curse. I was parentless by the age of 12, which totally changed the trajectory of my life. Surviving the premature death of my parents, rape and becoming a single mother at 31 caused me to lose my identity, trust and faith. Burdened with guilt and shame I existed a lot in life – more so than living. Having been raised in and around church, God is a constant, but when you feel like even God doesn't love or care for you, your hope vanishes. Admittedly, these were some of the hardest times in my life that contributed to me feeling like I was not enough.

On Easter of 1977, my mom died from an accidental gunshot wound. On Labor Day of 1982, my dad was robbed and killed. I missed my mom greatly, but my dad was great, having done everything to overcompensate for me and my siblings not having a mother. Within years of my mom's death, our childhood home burned, resulting in the loss of every baby picture and memory of our mom. When my Dad was killed, my life was not worth living; I felt like my whole world ended. I did not want to go on and I often prayed and asked God to take me. I was empty, angry, confused, lost and hurt to say the least. I got to see another side of love and it was nothing nice. I didn't really know what home was because my address changed frequently and sometimes without advance notice. I remember moving back from Ohio to my hometown and returning to school thinking things were back on track. However, one morning as my teacher was calling roll in homeroom, one of my classmates called me a Gypsy because he said all I did was move around from place to place. This comment cut deep because it was, for the most part, true. I had no permanent address and no sense of real identity anymore. This lack of identity led me to believe God didn't love me because I was not good enough.

During the moves, I suffered from various types of abuse, mostly sexual abuse from people who said they loved me. My abusers were people I trusted, who said they had love for me and my parents. Yet, their actions expressed the opposite of their words, so how could this be? One day in particular, a family friend took me on a motorcycle ride that turned into a devastating experience. What was supposed to be a simple joy ride turned into something so ugly. I wondered why things were happening to me as they were, and early on, I decided that maybe I deserved it. I had already lost my identity, and eventually, I began to lose my voice. I became a victim and the life I had known as a young girl with both parents still living was now a distant memory. I lost hope and didn't really care anymore. I just went along to get along, never telling anyone what I was going through because I didn't feel like anyone cared or would believe me. I even convinced myself that I had done something to cause everything to happen. My self-worth was in the pits! And again, I felt I was not good enough.

  Lastly, I remember being at a doctor's appointment when I was younger and being told by several specialists that I would never have children. The doctors even said that if I became pregnant, my body would not be able to carry the child. I wondered was this because of the things that had happened, or was I, again, somehow being punished. Over the years, I hoped and dreamed of having children but to no avail. After years of giving up on the thought of having a child, I started dating someone I had avoided for years. Things went well and everything continued to go well until something happened, or shall I say didn't happen. I was late! This was crazy; this had never happened. The thought of being pregnant was not in my plans, and it soon became apparent such was the same for the guy I was dating. When I shared the news, things took a turn for the worse as it became evident that I'd be raising my child alone. How could I survive everything that life had thrown at me only to become another statistic? Why couldn't he see that this baby was a miracle from God? Why couldn't he see me worthy enough to stick by my side? Why would God do this to me? I spent years condemning myself. I allowed other people's judgments to take up space in my head and my heart because even at the age of 31, I still didn't feel like I was good enough.

I want to encourage you, man or woman, if you've ever felt like you were not good enough, know that everything God made was and is good! Know that you are not only good, but You are Enough! I pray the following tips will prove life-changing on your journey to healing, forgiveness, and moving forward knowing You Are Enough:

1. First and foremost, it's important for you to stand in your truth. What really happened? How did you feel and how do you feel now?
2. Secondly, forgive yourself – make peace with your past and make peace with self because life didn't happen to you, life happened for you – and then others. Forgiveness will be required before you can move forward, but also know it is a process.
3. Seek God and work on building a relationship with him by reading and studying his word. The Bible provides all the instructions and guidance you need on your life's journey. Understand what it means

to surrender to his will knowing that his ways are not our ways and his will is not our will, but better and greater.

4. Find a church that teaches relationship versus religion. (As you grow, you will better understand this statement).

5. Be encouraged to press your way through, as it is written, "For I know the plans I have for you," declares the Lord, "plans to prosper you and not to harm you, plans to give you hope and a future." (Jeremiah 29:11, NIV) In other words, life may happen, but you must remember that God is the author and finisher of your fate. There will always be roadblocks, detours, valleys, traumas, life-altering situations and circumstances, but know that God will never leave nor forsake you. It is in your times of weakness that He is

made strong. You must be like Paul and understand that God's grace is sufficient. At times, it is hard to believe that a loving God allows you to go through so much, but it's important to lean not to your own understanding and in all your ways acknowledge Him. (Prov. 3:5-6, KJV)

6. Move forward on purpose with purpose.

Lastly, I want to encourage you to journal. Journaling should not be shared, as this will allow you to be honest. Journaling should flow freely, not guided or streamlined. Allow it to be an expression of your thoughts and feelings – good, bad and indifferent. You should journal consistently for at least six months with intention daily. Be sure not to "look back" before three months; this will allow you to see your growth. I want you to take back your power so you can take back your life! You will have to surrender, which will yield you vulnerable, but you will be forever changed in the process. You have to hurt before you can truly heal, but you have to be willing to heal in order to truly live!

I had to understand whose I am and who I am, so that I could know, realize and accept that I AM ENOUGH! When you know, realize and accept the same thing, you too, will know that YOU ARE ENOUGH and join me in saying,
"I Am Who God Says I Am, and I Am Living My Life on Purpose!"

My Reflections

I AM_____

I AM WHO GOD SAYS I AM

Debra Davis is a wife, mother of two and grandmother of two. She is the author of a new children's five book series called *Brianna's Dreams/I Just Want to Know*. She is also the Founder of two organizations, Debra's Dream Room and Ministering Women Ministering, Inc. She received two master's degrees (Master of Arts in Counseling and Master of Education in Adult Education) from the University of Arkansas at Little Rock. She worked as an AR Certified Trainer for the Early Childhood Education Program through the University of Arkansas at Fayetteville for six years. She also served as a motivational speaker for a Christian non-profit organization, Children of Arkansas Loved for a Lifetime, also known as C.A.L.L. She currently enjoys volunteering for community outreach programs, her local church Body of Christ Worship Center in Little Rock, Arkansas, and spending time with her grandchildren.

Email

debradavis2018@gmail.com

Website

www.debrasdreamroom.com

Phone Number

501-249-9732

Facebook

www.Facebook.com/debrasdreamroom

Instagram

www.instagram.com/debrasdreamroom

Twitter

www.twitter.com/hdebrasdreamroom

DEBRA'S DEDICATION

To those who struggle with moving forward because of adverse situations experienced.

DEBRA

I AM Evolving

How I evolved is similar to flying on an airplane; you board the plane, buckle your seat belt, and say a prayer asking God to safely take you on your journey, if it be his will. You feel the plane jerk forward as you hit some bumps on the tarmac as you your pilots prepare to take off. Those small bumps prepare you for some of the massive turbulence you will feel later in the flight. Like the turbulence you experience in a plane, this is how my life evolves.

Why I chose the word evolving you ask, the definition of the word, my childhood, and my experiences from my childhood embodies this definition in totality. This process helped me become a confident speaker, pursue my college degree, and be an attentive and loving parent to my two children. Webster's Dictionary defines the word "evolve" as a verb that means to develop gradually from a simple to a more advanced state (Merriam-Webster's Collegiate Dictionary, 2008). I believe evolution takes place when you are trying to move from point A to point B. In order to accomplish this, you must undergo a change in order to reach that higher level. God allows you to experience things in your life that changes your perspective and gives you the vision and spiritual wisdom that you need to ascend to that next level. God put me on a path where I would have to take action in order to fulfill and walk my purpose despite the ever-mounting adversities that constantly consumed my life.

My childhood was unusual, to say the least. At the age of four my biological mother tried to stuff me in a hot oven, but even in that traumatic event God provided a way of escape and I can boldly tell you the story today. After escaping that traumatic experience, I was adopted and raised in a small town of DeValls Bluff, Arkansas by my father, Henry Stidham, a barber who had an eighth-grade education and my mother, Sarah Stidham, a first-grade teacher. My mother taught school for 42 years. She was also a go-getter and a community leader. Despite not being able to know or establish a relationship with my biological parents, I was blessed to have a great childhood. My adopted mother inspired me to work hard in order to achieve my dreams and goals in my life. I watched how hard she would work to help the students that she taught every day and night.

Because of turbulence I had gone through in the beginning of my life, it took me awhile to get to the essence and core of me; due to the trauma I had experienced at such a young age. I was that child who lived her life in a cocoon for years even as an adult. I never felt good about myself because of the continued rejection I had gone through as a child, which contributed to a lot of the issues that transpired in childhood and carried themselves throughout my adult life. In spite of that abusive situation, I made the best of it and remained positive. I had childlike faith like the small mustard seed.

There was a time in my life that I was too afraid and too shy to speak in front of audiences. Since then, I have developed as a speaker by constantly reading a genre of books and using the dictionary app on my phone to sharpen my vocabulary skills while communicating to others. In order to keep confident in speaking in front of others, I constantly encourage myself and tell myself not to be afraid to speak at different speaking engagements. Now, I am requested to speak at multiple events, and I enjoy sharing my experience about how God used my experiences of pain and brokenness in order to help others.

Because I wanted to be a better person, I was determined to pursue my goal of finishing college. The first time I went to college, I did not take my education seriously. Because I did not take my education seriously, I flunked my first semester of college with a 1.75 grade point average (GPA). Later, I decided that I needed to go back to school, so I worked very hard when I was given a second chance to attend college again. I worked on purpose, and I made A's and B's during my second chance of attending college. I knew that I evolved while pursuing my education because the goal that I set before graduation was reached. I graduated not only with two master's degrees, but I earned a 3.33 GPA. I followed in my mother's footsteps when she pursued her college degree and was the first in her family to obtain her degree.

Looking back over the experience of attending college and pursuing my degree helped me be an attentive and loving parent to my two children. I wanted my children to see through my example that despite the odds that seem to be against you, you can still accomplish your goals in life. I did not develop or pick up any bad habits from my biological mother known to me because she wasn't involved in my life during my childhood.

I came to realize that the approaches for discipline that she used were not appropriate, and I didn't use those strategies to rear my children because how she disciplined me is considered child abuse and neglect. The approaches that my mother used to discipline me were spankings out of control, beatings, or burning or bruising my skin. My approach that I used to help discipline my children were to teach them that they had to make good choices, and if not, there would be consequences for their actions whether disobeying the rules at home or at school. I gave them examples of the consequences that would happen for not obeying from a biblical standard and a real-life standard which was breaking the law.

    In essence, every parent hopes their child learns from his or her mistakes. One thing that I have learned from rearing my children is that you must pray and continue to do your best to help them until they are grown. I still remember this saying that my parents would often quote to me, "After everything is said and done, the choices which you make right or wrong does not fall on us as your parent any longer, it falls on you my child."

In spite of what I've been through, I am evolving into the person that God has planned and purposed me to be.

I AM

Favored

Enough

Evolving

Fearless

Restored

Chosen

Found

Resilient

An Overcomer

I am who GOD says I AM.

LIVING MY LIFE ON PURPOSE

My Reflections

IAM _____

I AM WHO GOD SAYS I AM

Jennifer Nsenkyire is an author, speaker and advocate for Sickle Cell Disease (SCD) and other chronic diseases. She was born and raised in Ghana, West Africa and migrated to the US in 1997. After being cured of both SCD and Multiple Sclerosis (MS), Jennifer, penned her memoir titled, *My Pool of Bethesda: A Place of Healing and Transformation*, to share her journey. The transformation of Jennifer's life through Stem Cell Transplantation in 2010 is the impetus for her work as a speaker and an advocate for individuals and/or families with loved ones who suffer from SCD and other chronic diseases. Her memoir has impacted the lives of many.

Jennifer is the current Vice President for the Fredericksburg Area Sickle Cell Association (FASCA). Her hobbies include singing, playing chess and scrabble. She is also a graduate of George Mason University with a Bachelor of Science in Finance.

E-mail jenn.nsenkyire@gmail.com

Website

www.jennifernsenkyire.com

Phone

540-987-6455

Facebook

www.facebook.com/JenniferNsenkyire

Instagram

www.instagram.com/mypoolofbethesda

Twitter

www.twitter.com/ JNsenkyire

JENNIFER'S DEDICATION

To patients suffering from chronic diseases and their families, be fearless!

JENNIFER'S ACKNOWELDGEMENT

Kiesha L. Peterson – the visionary author of this project - thank you for your mentorship.

JENNIFER'S TRIBUTE

In Honor of
Maame Yaa Gyamfuah

LIVING MY LIFE ON PURPOSE

JENNIFER

I AM Fearless

Having been born to Rose and Edward Osei Nsenkyire from Ghana, West Africa, I was not your typical child. I began facing medical challenges a little over a year after my birth. Although my family attempted to make life as normal as possible for me, their attempts would be that of an uphill climb. With my faith, love and support of family and friends around me, I have and will continue to overcome challenges thrown my way for I am fearless.

Being Fearless is coping with chronic pain for over 37 years. Learning to live through pain on a daily basis began as an infant. At that tender age I did not understand nor grasp the extent of what I was feeling. It broke my mother's heart each time she helplessly observed me in an episode of pain crises. It was even more devastating once my parents began to seek answers to gain a better understanding of my symptoms. Their search revealed a glimpse of the fight that was ahead of me. I was diagnosed with Sickle Cell Disease (SCD) and my genotype was SS. This genotype SS meant I had inherited the hemoglobin S gene from each parent.

Being Fearless is not giving up even when told at a young age my condition of SCD would affect me gravely; that I may not live to see my 21st birthday. Yet, my parents chose not to give up, but rather sought answers to understand the condition in order to properly adjust our lifestyle. I knew what the triggers of my pain episodes were and could often tell the onset of a crisis. Every time we thought we had discovered a solution to help limit the frequency of the pain crises, we would be thrown a curve ball. Sometimes it felt as though it was the first time I was experiencing such pain. The pain would manifest in different ways, sometimes leaving me bed ridden for months. Most days I often thought to myself, 'How can I live a normal life when I am constantly in pain?' Over time, pain became my normal. SCD complicated my life and imposed on my desire to live a normal life. Yet, with the support of my family and in leaning on my faith, I did not give up.

Being Fearless is being brave to attempt walking after being bedridden for six months. I conquered my fear of not being able to walk again when I believed that indeed the Lord reveals to redeem. At nine years old, I survived Osteomyelitis, a bone infection that affected my limbs. All four limbs were placed in a cast leaving me bedridden. The fear of not knowing whether my legs would buckle or sustain my weight crippled me. I never thought I'd be able to walk again; yet, when I faced my fears and stepped out in faith, I did indeed walk again. I'd had a revelation in the form of a dream after reading the scripture Acts 3:6. This dream was revealing and impactful on my life. In the dream I was asleep in my hospital bed when I felt someone come into my room and touch me.

The touch was soft and gentle, like that of a feather. Even though this touch was like the brush of a feather, it felt as though it was one intended to wake me up. As I opened my eyes, I saw a man standing at the foot of my bed. The man looked like Jesus with long hair and facial features often depicted in the Bible stories I had read. He looked at me with a gentle smile and said, "Jennifer, can you walk?" It was as if I knew this man from before. I was not in the least bit afraid and calmly answered "Yes." He extended his arm and said, "Jennifer get up and walk." I got up slowly out of the bed and walked towards him. Somehow the casts and bandages had fallen off my limbs. No longer seeing the limitations and hindrances, I also no longer felt fear.

Being Fearless is coping with a debilitating autoimmune disease. By coping I sought refuge in the Lord. Being diagnosed with Multiple Sclerosis (MS) was a shock, and I could not fathom living with both SCD and MS. However, God gave me the strength to face each day no matter how difficult it became. I was fearless in choosing to self-inject to control the MS symptoms. The first year after diagnosis was the most difficult; however, I learned to embrace it and resigned myself to the fact that this was the hand I had been dealt and was unwillingly going to live with it the best way I could.

Being Fearless is surviving a six-day coma. This coma was a result of complications from a blood transfusion and medication and could have resulted in my demise. With my family by my side, I fought for my life and God saw me through this coma. I resisted the urge to quit fighting. However, let me also share that being fearless is overcoming addiction. I struggled for many years with addiction to prescription medications. Although I needed these medications to cope with the pain, overtime, it became an escape from the emotional pain. I became depressed and often wished on many nights I would not wake up to face another day. The addiction to pain medicine turned me into a person I am not proud of. My family was bearing the brunt of my anger and frustration. Like any addict, I would never admit nor accept I was an addict although my gut feeling said otherwise.

Being Fearless is overcoming insecurities. The feeling of worthlessness and being incapable of accomplishing tasks and goals consumed me. The more I dwelled on this, the more depressed, lonelier and angrier I became. I overcame my insecurities when I learned to let go and trust God. I took a leap of faith when the opportunity for Stem Cell Transplantation (SCT) was offered. Knowing the risks and uncertainties involved in SCT, I was still willing to take a chance. It turned out to be very successful, as I was now cured of both diseases.

Being Fearless is finding your purpose in life. I knew God healed me for a reason, as I eventually published my memoir: *My Pool of Bethesda: A Place of Transformation and Healing* in 2018 – a story of inspiration and encouragement to others with similar life experiences. If something I've shared above resonates with you, I leave you with these final words of encouragement:

1. Do not isolate yourself, which is easy to do when you are faced with an unexpected diagnosis or situation. It is natural to want to be alone as you digest the news. However, this is the time to surround yourself with people who love you as you make sense of the situation.
2. Surround yourself with folks who are prayerful with steadfast faith. These are the folks you can call and lean on heavily for prayers and strength when the going gets tough.
3. Understand, nothing catches God by surprise. He knows us individually and knows everything we are going through. He has orchestrated every step in

our lives. Jeremiah 29:11 reminds us that God has good plans for us. Though it may not seem like it is a good plan at the moment, be reminded that it will all work out for your benefit and for His Glory.

4. Allow yourself permission to cry if you need to. Allow yourself permission to vent and be angry at God for the hand you have been dealt. He can take it. It is in our raw moments that we're able to reveal our deepest hurts and challenges. However, do not dwell and wallow in that space for too long. Just pass through it and walk out into your Strong Tower (Proverbs 18:10), who is our God. Know there is nothing too difficult for Him, and in His time, he will make it all better.

When you feel fearful, anxious or worried about your trials and tribulations, your struggles in life, know that is the work of the enemy. The enemy wants to prevent you from living fearlessly. Do not fret! Step out in faith! The enemy will attempt to keep you in that space so he can watch your dreams and aspirations wither. He will stifle the plans God has for you by taking a hold of your thoughts and feed it lies.

With faith, prayer and supplication, you can turn things around by seeking God. As you meditate and ponder on God's word, it will take control over your thoughts and your heart. As you surrender and pray, the Holy Spirit will take over and as it resides in you, it changes you from the inside out. As you start to believe what the Bible says about God's promises for your life and how he has ultimate control and power over everything, you'll begin to experience a transformation of your mind.

Keep your eyes on God no matter what you may be facing. He will give you the courage and strength you need to face what you're enduring.

Be fearless my fellow brothers and sisters just as God asks us to be in Joshua 1:9, for He is with us wherever we go.

I AM

Favored

Enough

Evolving

Fearless

Restored

Chosen

Found

Resilient

An Overcomer

I am who GOD says I AM.

LIVING MY LIFE ON PURPOSE

My Reflections

I AM _____

I AM WHO GOD SAYS I AM

Juanita Gaynor is a Philadelphia native who relocated to Atlanta, GA in 2008, where she began her event planning career at age fourteen. She is a certified wedding planner who holds Associates' degrees in Business Administration from Eastern Nazarene College and Accounting from Atlanta Technical College.

A prolific entrepreneur, Juanita has the following organizations:

- EABJ Consulting and Event Management, Inc., a special event and meeting management company.
- Restored 2 Life, a non-profit organization working with survivors of child abuse.
- Elite Financial Management LLC, a full services accounting and bookkeeping firm that evaluates your individual needs to customize the best accounting solution for your business.

- Moving Past You Radio Show to help identify, confront and embrace obstacles that block and delay our walking in divine purpose.

E-mail

connect@juanitaegaynor.com

Website

www.juanitaegaynor.com

Phone

678-225-8939

Facebook

www.facebook.com/**JuanitaEGaynor**

Instagram

www.instagram.com/juanitaegaynor

Twitter

www.twitter.com/juanitaegaynor

JUANITA'S TRIBUTE

In Honor of

Dora Mae Sandlin

No longer afraid or ashamed. I am finally living in purpose on purpose!

JUANITA

I AM Restored

For I know the thoughts that I think toward you, saith the Lord, thoughts of peace, and not of evil, to give you an expected end. Jeremiah 29:11 (KJV)

I am Philly girl born and raised. I was born Juanita Estell Anastacia Marie Price Gaynor on Friday December 13, 1974 in Philadelphia, Pennsylvania to Viola Mae Gaynor & Charles Noah Price, Sr. I was my father's only daughter and my mother's third child. Even early on from what I remember, trouble always seemed to ensue. Amidst the trouble, my father did what he could in attempting to get custody. Back then, men were not considered to be suitable care givers, so I stayed with my mother. Music was the one certain and calming constant in my life. I remember it always playing, my mother singing and it always giving hope that the next day would be better than the last one. Three years later, in the winter of 1977, my younger brother would come into the mix and all hell broke loose. Up to this point, my mother had done a really good job at disguising her addiction, but now it was out in the open on full display spinning crazily out of control. She could no longer function day to day and her neglect of us only intensified. There were nights I spent praying for reprieve or rescue, but in the silence of the night, it always felt that no one could hear the loud, silent cries.

I AM WHO GOD SAYS I AM

I always knew I was different; I never was able to explain why, but I was. I was attuned to my delight in praise and worship and my ability to minister in song even at a young age. But there was an ever-present spirit that was trying to kill that desire and to permanently shut down what God had put in me. At the time, I was too young to understand or to kill it myself. The enemy used the portal that was my mother's addiction to do his dirty work for him.

I remember there being many times my mother beat me because I would try to always protect my baby brother. In doing so, I got the brunt of the abuse. We would have some goods days but for me, the bad far outweighed the good. My mother was a drug addict and her drug of choice was Heroin. She had her ups and downs and I had become numb to the roller coaster's constant twists, turns and sudden, often deadly stops. However, one day that all changed for the worst; the world and innocence I knew disappeared forever. My mother was coming down hard off her latest high and on this particular day, she did not have any money to pay her dealer for her next high. On that day, I became her currency. The dealers and the pimps did not care that I was a child; they all were getting what they wanted and more. My mother did not have the capacity to care because to alleviate and obliterate her pain, she placed me in pain. On that day, I learned a lesson that would alter my life course for many years to come, I learned women are fickle and cannot be trusted and that sex was just a means to an end. I was five years old.

The beatings by my mother continued and the sexual abuse escalated. Not only was I being abuse by the dealer and pimps, I was being abused by those whose houses we stayed in because they felt it was a fair trade for having a roof over our head and them allowing us to eat.

Abuse was so engrained in my being that is was normal. When I visited my grandmother and no one bothered me, I was able to sleep in my room in peace. Ironically, I thought they were strange and weird. What I did not understand at the time was I was never supposed to be exposed to what I had been exposed to at such a young age.

    I remember the last beating from my mother like it was yesterday. She was coming down off a major high. She had no money to get her next fix and this particular dealer made it very clear he was not going to touch me because that was not how be rolled. When he left cementing the fact that she would not be getting any drugs that night, she directed all her disappointment and rage towards me. This beating was unlike any other. She was in an uncontrollable raged. She slammed my hands in the doors, tried to burn them on the stove and beat me with whatever she could get her hands on. She finally passed out on the bed. For me, that marked when it all ended. I fixed my brother dinner as he was crying hysterically. I remember telling him everything would be okay. I prepared him for bed that evening, getting all his snacks and toys together. I instructed him not to come from behind that partition. I also told him he was only to do so if I or the police came to get him. He started crying again. I was black and blue. I had no more tears left and I no longer cared. I had decided this would be the last time she was going to hit me. I found her machete, sat on her chest and waited hours for her to wake up. When she awoke, she was startled as of course, she did not remember what had happened hours before. As I sat on her chest, I pressed the machete as hard as I could against her neck, but it would not cut her. When it did not cut her, I warned her that if she ever hit us again, I would kill her.

Later that day, she dropped us off at a friend's house. That was the last time I saw her alive. The year was 1983 and I was eight years old.

It would be years later when I would finally understand that God was in the situation all along. Even with the ups and downs, the long incidents of depression and post-traumatic stress disorder episodes, God had ordered my steps. Even in the lowest times, He was there. Even when I wanted to throw in the towel, He gave me a peace that surpassed my own understanding. God restored my child-like faith so that I would be able to follow Him and soar to heights unknown.

Never give up, never quit; your purpose is too great, and you are too valuable to God and the kingdom.

The Lord is my shepherd; I shall not want. He maketh me to lie down in green pastures: he leadeth me beside the still waters. He restoreth my soul: he leadeth me in the paths of righteousness for his name's sake. Yea, though I walk through the valley of the shadow of death, I will fear no evil: for thou art with me; thy rod and thy staff they comfort me. Thou preparest a table before me in the presence of mine enemies: thou anointest my head with oil; my cup runneth over. Surely, goodness and mercy shall follow me all the days of my life: and I will dwell in the house of the Lord forever. Psalm 23 (KJV)

I AM

Favored

Enough

Evolving

Fearless

Restored

Chosen

Found

Resilient

An Overcomer

I am who GOD says I AM.

My Reflections

I AM _____

I AM WHO GOD SAYS I AM

LIVING MY LIFE ON PURPOSE

Kocysha LaShaun is a long-time resident of Central Arkansas where she completed a Bachelor's program in Criminal Justice Administration and an online Master's program in Forensic Psychology. The opportunity to work as a Correctional Officer and College Instructor are two of her greatest professional accomplishments.

In 2013, she became a self-taught transcriptionist and authored her first book, *Humbled by His Grace*. In late 2018, she self-published *Out of the Darkness, and Into the LIGHT*, as the first of a mini-book series. In early 2019, Kocysha completed the Black Belt Speakers Training, became a Certified Life, Success, and Empowerment Coach; and restructured Be Accelerated into Purpose (BAIP), her teacher/trainer, coach/consulting business to now focus on personal, spiritual, and professional development for other solopreneurs and business/ministry leaders.

On a personal note, Kocysha, is a long-time listener of K-Love, an avid reader of self-help and inspirational books, and a long-time fan of crime shows.

E-mail
Kocyshalashaun@gmail.com
Website
https://kocyshalashaun.wixsite.com/baip
Phone
501-764-2881
Facebook
www.facebook.com/kocyshalashaun
Twitter
www.twitter.com/kocyshalashaun

KOCYSHA'S DEDICATION

To the men and women who feel forgotten or overlooked. You're Not!!! You've simply been hidden and Set Apart as His Chosen!

KOCYSHA

I AM Chosen

At times you've wondered and even questioned, 'When is my time?' Or you've been in situations of opportunity where you've thought, 'Here I am! Pick me!' Or maybe you've pondered, 'What am I missing? Am I not connecting with the right people?' I'm willing to bet it hasn't been an easy journey. In fact, it's seemed quite isolating, lonely, and even a bit unfulfilled. Well, believe it or not, I understand! I understand because even with three degrees, even having excelled academically and professionally, I too, have found myself asking these same questions of God which then led to some heavy self-reflection questions.

So, allow me to share with you three experiences that revealed great lessons of insight on how God grooms us, teaches us, and prepares us for our specific, CHOSEN assignment(s). More importantly, these experiences helped me realize that feeling forgotten and overlooked was indeed a figment of my carnal imagination. You may not feel that way now, but as you continue to read, I pray there will be a stirring in your spirit that convinces you otherwise.

While working at a cancer clinic between 2001 and 2007, I received Employee of the Month twice and Employee of the Year once, with the latter being the first and, I think, the only time it had ever been awarded. But one month, it went to someone else when I just knew I would get it. I'm not sure why it was such an issue **this** particular month as this was done many, many times. I just remember the next day, I was ticked, and it reflected in my attitude. But why?

I remember receiving an email near the end of a Friday workday announcing a supervisor position and I was super excited about it. Over the weekend, I typed out a proposal, even placing it into a report cover. Monday morning came and I was set to meet with the head attorney that afternoon. I walked into her office confident with my proposal in hand. Unfortunately, I never got to present it as I was told they were choosing someone else, but there was still a possibility for me in the near future once I learned two other desk assignments. Can I be honest? It took everything in me not to tear up and combat their choice of a person who in my eyes, was in the same boat as me. The person was not really sociable and also still needed to learn particular desk assignments, etc. Yes, it was a blow to my pride because in all honesty, I was not really used to being told 'no' because of what I didn't know. Yes, I felt defeated because I believed it didn't matter what I lacked in experience; God would work it out. When it didn't happen as I'd thought, yes there were questions! And eventually, God answered and reminded me of something I'd forgotten and lost sight of.

EVEN at the age of 40, I found myself anticipating hearing my name for an award. I was in attendance at a three-day training event and on the last day, selected persons give away an award to those with significant stories or messages to share. This was the second time within the year I'd attended. At the first event, I watched all other first-time attendees receive one, but not me. I literally felt small, wanting to retreat under a rock as I clapped for each, congratulated them, and took their pics. I was a bit hurt and wondered how the point person at my table awarded everyone BUT me. At the second event, I thought I'd definitely receive one, having briefly shared my story of promiscuity. But that was not the case. I think the first two hours of that 8-hour drive back home, I had to have a 'come to Jesus talk' with my own self. I had to ask myself some hard questions. It troubled me even when I got home because I knew this was something I had to shake: the need to be recognized and validated. I prayed about it and over time God began to make it super clear through a few sermons and passages of how He works and why.

Now comes the moment of self-reflection: Why was I so upset that a co-worker was selected for Employee of the Month? Why was I so upset that I did not get the promotion at work? And why was I so upset that I wasn't selected for an award? The simple answer to each is that I selfishly made it about 'me': what 'I' wanted and what 'I' felt I deserved.

When I changed my perspective, when I began to 'See Self as God Sees', when I got truthful with self, as I hope you will, these were the insights gained:

1. As 'We Are Chosen', we have to be willing to share the limelight. In fact, there will be more times than not when we not only have to share it, but willingly step away from, and out of it.

2. If the work ethic we exemplify, the sacrifices and contributions we make are really for the glory of God, we would not be the least bit concerned about personal recognition.

3. Sometimes we don't get a promotion because we want it for selfish reasons and have lost focus of what God has already instructed or shown us. The rejection is not meant to make us feel less than or unworthy.

Rejection can serve as a reminder that what we want is not what God wants or has in store for us.

4. Sometimes, we have to get real with self and truly assess the validity of our frustrations with others, and why we feel we are more deserving or can do a better job than someone else. Many of us have a tendency to reflect personal frustrations onto others. Could it be that our frustration with someone else's seemingly lack of is really a frustration with self and the excuses we've been making?

The truth is we're all Chosen – chosen to fulfill a purpose, chosen to walk a set path already created, chosen to serve a specific group of people in a specific place at a specific time. That's Good News! Actually, it's Great News! The unfortunate thing, however, is we allow our insecurities and fears to distort spiritual insight with what we see in the physical.

I want to leave you with something I believe that really reflects how God works and why: *"Then I heard the voice of the Lord saying, "Whom will I send and who will go for us?" And I said, "Here am I. Send me!" He said, "Go and tell this people..."* (Isaiah 6:8-9a, NIV). *Barak said to her, "If you go with me, I will go, but if you don't go with me, I won't go." "Very well," Deborah said, I will go with you. But because of the way you are going about this, the honor will not be yours, for the Lord will hand Sisera over to a woman."* (Judges 3:8-9a, NIV).

When He asks, "Whom will I send and who will go for us?" That's you! That's me! His Chosen Ones. He doesn't demand us to go; He gives us a choice. And many of us say "Yes," not realizing that along with that yes comes a process. We think things will happen suddenly, but that's not always the case depending on where we are spiritually. See once we say 'Yes,' then God begins to groom us for an assignment that many of us are still clueless about if we're honest. But His grooming and growth processes can come in the form of situations that include some form of rejection or tearing down of our carnal desires. It can come through a relationship, work, or by way of another avenue.

Please don't let this pass you by: While you think you're forgotten or being overlooked; God has simply hidden you so He can prepare you. When He sends you where no one else will go, when He calls on you to be the voice for others, when He assigns you to speak to the nations, when He appoints you to bless lives and win souls, He needs to know He can trust you to do so for HIS GLORY and not your own. He needs to know that when you go out, you no longer will be thrown off emotionally when people reject you or when support is none to minimal. He needs to know that you're giving and doing without selfish expectations, but rather, that it is in obedience and willingness in fulfilling your purpose in Him. The Greatest Reward ever is in knowing that where you go, God will always sustain you because You Are Chosen – anointed and appointed for something greater beyond your imagination or current circumstance.

I AM

Favored
Enough
Evolving
Fearless
Restored
Chosen
Found
Resilient
An Overcomer

I am who GOD says I AM.

My *Reflections*

*I AM*_____

I AM WHO GOD SAYS I AM

Despite mistakes, mishaps and disobediences, God saw fit to call **Michelle** a "minister who happens to…" and she answers the call. Ms. **Flagg** is a proud mother and grandmother who is driven to live life by the dictates of who God originally intended for her to be. Also known as The Genesis Woman, Michelle has been described as real and giving, with a desire to see women authentically succeed. "It's not about being equal to or better than a man. It's about being who God has equipped you to be without shame or apology, as a woman". Michelle is an author, speaker, editor and creative transcriber of words in multiple formats. At this juncture in her life, she holds three practices to heart. First, know and love God. Second, have a healthy relationship with self. Third, give from the best of who you really are.

Email

thegenesiswomanministries@gmail.com

LIVING MY LIFE ON PURPOSE

MICHELLE'S TRIBUTE

In memory of

Robert Lee Hargrove, Jr.

and

Eva Dell King Hargrove

The legacy to reverence God and "fear no man", continues. Thank you.

MICHELLE

I AM Found

I was very young when I began to realize that I carried a nagging feeling as though I didn't belong. As part of the migrating population north for better job opportunities in the 50s, my parent's work ethic was fierce, and they erred on the side of being old-fashioned when it came to raising me. I am the oldest and only girl of three siblings. I learned to live within the cultural confines they placed on me. I was a good girl who never caused problems. I was polite and personable. As expected, I excelled in school. From the outside, it appeared I fared well. But on the inside, I was conflicted. I wanted to join the Girl Scouts. We didn't have the money. I wanted to take ballet lessons. "We" didn't do those kinds of things. I wanted to go to the neighborhood recreation center after school. I had to help care for my oldest brother. To let my parents tell it, I always wanted things that were beyond my reach. I moved away from home, but I never saw what proved to be two of the greatest influencers in my life moving right along with me. My parents 'can not's and do not's' had taken root while merging with the 'American Dream'. What a paradoxical combination to base one's identity and purpose on!

When I landed a job at a major telecommunications corporation, quite a few people were oddly pleased. I just wanted to do my job well. I progressed from my beginnings as a word processor to promotion into a project supervisor position. The job perks were advantageous; my salary exceeded what I know some make today! It was at my fifteen-year mark where the tide took an unexpected turn. Based on my service and age, I had nine years to retirement. The industry landscape and competition weren't accommodating. The financial crisis was erupting in certain pockets in the country. Hiring practices had moved out of brick-n-mortar facilities to dot com addresses only. My retirement morphed into involuntary separation. I woke up the day after my last official day on the company payroll feeling lost and dumped. All I thought I knew no longer existed. By this time, I had been divorced for almost ten years. I couldn't help but note the eerie similarity of feeling between the two.

I searched for jobs like a dog hunting for a bone over the next two years. I was between the overqualified rock and the, "We're sorry, but you don't have your degree" hard place. I had never missed a mortgage payment. When two consecutive payments weren't made, the bank-initiated foreclosure. It was August 2003. I was born, married and divorced in August. I didn't need another life-changing experience to take place in August. I certainly felt I could have taken a pass on this one. In the recesses of my heart and mind, I was beyond lost. I thought the tide had turned concerning my career. What I didn't know was a tsunami was gearing up and heading toward me.

Within a period of less than ninety days, starting in August 2003 and ending in October 2003, the unimaginable happened. The first call came in from North Carolina. My father experienced complications resulting from a stroke and he had died. I sat and thought about that for a long time. My relationship with my father hadn't been what I would have liked. It took submission to God's divine and healing intervention to help me accept his human *being*, honor his undeniable position and to genuinely love him. I was grateful I had forgiven him. God assured me and I was thankful in knowing he was at rest. On the twenty-fifth day after his death, a second call came in. This time, the call came from Georgia. Once the doctor identified himself, he began explaining that my mom was in the hospital bleeding internally. I heard three things above everything else. The bleeding couldn't be stopped. She would experience pain if kept on life support. It was not expected she would live into the night. My brothers and I hadn't even reached the halfway point between Indiana and Georgia when she died. I will never forget the declaration I made when they told me she died. I fell to my knees, gasping and screaming in the same breath. I told God I could not lose another thing.

I believe my childhood distresses with my parents' beliefs on gender and race was something God used to keep truth simmering inside of me. Before all was said and done, I had to unlearn and lose certain beliefs to take hold of some vital truths. My parents didn't know everything, and they weren't perfect. But in God's infinite wisdom, they were perfect for me. They each loved me based on their perceived definitions of love. While some of the methodologies were convoluted, collectively they left me a legacy that will serve me for the rest of my life.

Loss can sometimes be beneficial. When I lost the prestigious job, I lost the facades and fallacies that it carried. I had allowed it to become my identity. What was surprising was that others had too! I can't tell you how many friends quickly vanished into thin air when that job ended.

Losing something you've dreamed of and worked to obtain can be devastating. When it's a house, it can be debilitating. I walked through days, weeks, months and yes, years refusing to even consider buying a house again. I had done the right things but to what end? Well, a house is a thing. Most things can be replaced. Going through foreclosure didn't kill me. It knocked me down. It definitely carried its own set of challenges. I can honestly say I gained a meaningful understanding from the experience. A house is not a home. God is my home.

When I mention in conversation that my parents died in 2003, people assume it was the result of an accident. I suppose it's a logical assumption to make. After all, whose parents die twenty-five days apart? To this day, I don't know if there is any significance to that fact. What I know is this

- It is sobering to realize that the two people who loved you first are no longer on this side of eternity living somewhere on the planet. An even better degree of sobriety comes from knowing I am not an orphan left alone in this world. God is indeed Abba and He loves me always.

Typically, the subject of loss generally escapes our conversations. I am convinced that loss is an intricate part of life's cycle. For every loss I've had, I've received gain I couldn't have foreseen. When I began to recognize that, I thought it strange at first. But God's ways are higher than ours. While I was in a state of loss, feeling utterly lost, I saw His desire for my life.

Matthew 10:39 states: *Anyone who finds his life will lose it, and anyone who loses his life because of Me will find it* (Christian Standard Bible). As a believer, ownership of my life, its purpose, passion, and calling doesn't originate from me. Neither does it belong to me. It belongs to Christ. Who better to define who I am than Him? My identity, value, and worth are priceless to Him. Every surrender and obedience to God's will and plans for me ultimately prove to be what is absolutely best for me. His word tells me I can be and do all things He calls for through Christ, guaranteed. I don't have to try to figure it out. I don't have to try to fit in to be accepted. I don't even have to try to convince others to be understood. I am found in Christ. That is far greater than any perceived loss, guaranteed.

LIVING MY LIFE ON PURPOSE

My Reflections

I AM _____

I AM WHO GOD SAYS I AM

LIVING MY LIFE ON PURPOSE

Montell McClain was born and raised in Rocky Mount, NC. She was an early childhood professional before shifting to writing, humanitarianism and motivational speaking. She currently resides in Raleigh, NC and has four children and two grandchildren. Montell has an Associate's Degree in Early Childhood Education from Wake Technical Community College and a Bachelor's Degree in Child Development from Walden University.

She is a member of "Sigma Alpha Pi" National Society of Leadership and Success. She is currently working on starting a nonprofit organization for disadvantaged individuals, helping to pave a way to a brighter future. Montell has a love for reading and is working on coordinating a family literacy program. She's hoping that one of the many children's books she has written will be on the shelves in her program.

Her book collaborations include Amazon best sellers *The Pieces of My*

Platform and *Affirmations & Antidotes That Inspire Me.*

E-mail
lpride411@gmail.com

MONTELL'S DEDICATION

To My Children and Grandchildren

MONTELL'S ACKNOWLEDGEMENTS

Thank you Dr. Marilyn Porter and Minister Kiesha Peterson for believing in me.

MONTELL'S TRIBUTE

In Honor of
my Father

William McClain

MONTELL

I AM Resilient

I was born in Rocky Mount, North Carolina. I was an only child reared by my father and paternal grandparents. Born prematurely at six months old, I weighed one pound and six ounces. I had a praying grandmother and she stayed by my side until I was able to come home. Even at birth, God had given me the strength to get through life's difficulties. It seems God infused resiliency in my DNA.

I have overcome challenges all my life. Jeremiah 1:5 states: *"Before I formed you in the womb, I knew you, before you were born, I set you apart"*. God knew everything about me before I was even born. He knew my mother would abscond from my life at the beginning. He knew my Grandmother Irene - my angel and beacon of hope - would pass away when I was twelve years old. God knew my favorite aunt, Joyce, would move away when I was fifteen. Ultimately, various relationships would tear my father away too.

I can remember spending many holidays alone because my father and grandfather were gone. My mother didn't come around when I was younger, and I always felt out of place and alone. In the summertime, I would end up in Washington, D.C with a great aunt until summer was over. I enjoyed my time there, but I felt like a charity case.

I yearned to belong to a stable, close knit family. I wanted to feel like I was really part of the family especially around the holidays and during vacations. I still remember the Thanksgivings with no dinner and the Christmases with no presents. Had I been forgotten? I wanted that motherly love I had been missing, that certain type of love I believe shows us how to maneuver in this world. Even with the love my grandmother instilled in me from the beginning, I was still longing for a love I believed I needed. Because of this experience, I was determined as a mother that my children would not experience the same. I made sure my children were always together during the holidays. Even if it meant that I went without, I pulled through for them.

It was very important to me that my children felt loved because I knew what searching for love can cost. I got caught up in soul and emotional ties that left me tangled and more lost and confused. Missing motherly love and the intuitiveness that that love brings landed me in relationships with mates who were just as broken as I was.

By the time I was thirty years old, I was a mother of four who had experienced so many toxic, dysfunctional relationships, I was left feeling wrung out. I clung to one that I remained in for years. Those years has embedded some bitter memories. They consisted of repeated patterns of evictions, utilities being shut off, and a lack of food and necessities. This relationship left a gaping hole in my hedge of protection; because I began losing my faith. The enemy knew I had become weak and vulnerable and he would attack my finances repeatedly. There was always a financial lack. I am afflicted with pain because of memories my children shared of their childhood. There were good memories, but there were some that were not so good. I had dealt with so many traumatic experiences in my life that I had begun to compartmentalize them in my mind. There are a lot of things I do not remember but at times, subconscious residue will surface. My partner was not a provider, nor a man of faith in God. I remember one time, I asked him to pray. The retort was so sharp, it stung me. I became adaptable to this union, but deep inside I knew I needed a man of faith. I needed a man who could provide for me and my family, who was a prayer warrior, and someone who believed in the passions and purpose I held in my heart. I needed someone who would make me feel safe and not afraid. I would ask myself, "How can you be in a loveless relationship for all of these years?" The same man that I had spent years building up, was bit by bit tearing down the woman that I had become. The verbal abuse had become habitual and the norm of conversation. Each word that spewed from his mouth chipped away a piece of me. I would look that demon entity in its face as I stood in the whole armor of God. I would stand and plead the blood of Jesus as I asked God to contend with those who contend with me. After each verbal fight, I would spiritually pick up the pieces of me that he had torn with the words from his mouth. I would get on my knees and cry out to God to give me strength to weather this storm and to make it through. My Heavenly Father let me see what I thought was a rejection all of those years, was really divine redirection so that I could begin to walk into my calling.

The enemy had attempted at many stages of my life to break me, but I was not designed to break, and neither are you. We may bend and sometimes sway, but tie a knot in your rope and hang on. God has given us the resiliency and the ability to recover from difficulties. We must trust

Him. I learned early in life to seek the Lord and His strength. Seeking Him incessantly gave me strength and the staying power to continue in alignment with Christ. During my life's trials and tribulations, I still praised God and gave Him the glory. I knew God's goodness and mercy would carry me all the days of my life. It gave me the power of endurance to be content even during my storms. I knew that *"Ye are of God, little children, and have overcome them: because greater is he that is in you, than he that is in the world"* and I could make it and not fail. Philippians 4:11-12 states, *"Not that I am speaking of being in need, for I have learned in whatever situation I am to be content. I know how to be brought low, and I know how to abound. In any and every circumstance, I have learned the secret of facing plenty and hunger, abundance and need"*. Even when life has a path far different from the one we believe and desire, we must keep our eyes on Christ. He will direct our path. As an adult, I came to understand that my definition of love is different from God's. When I learned that God is Love, I was able to draw from the suppleness and durability of resilience to overcome life's challenges. When you have that feeling that I use to have, wanting to belong; realize that we have no conditions placed on God's love for us. God gives us unconditional love and enables us to withstand and heal from any situation. I am who God says I am; I am resilient.

My *Reflections*

I AM _____

I AM WHO GOD SAYS I AM

Sharifa A. Stirgus is a devoted wife of 19 years to Shon, and mother of two daughters, Alayah and Jayla, whom she loves to spend time with watching movies. She also loves to write and cook for family gatherings as well as serving and helping others where needed.

She received her Associates of Science Degree and certificate of Pre-Health Care Studies from Pulaski Technical College and is currently a Certified Phlebotomist of 21 years.

Sharifa is an overcomer, a light in the darkness, strong and loving. She understands the pain of women, and it is for this reason she is eager to speak to the hearts of young and older women who have been discouraged in their past, or who may be going through a difficult time in life. She is also passionate about helping others overcome fear and persecutions encountered from past or present situations.

E-mail

sharifa.stirgus@gmail.com

SHARIFA'S DEDICATION

To women who struggle with fear, bullying, and being heard.
I thank God who is forever loving and trustworthy, having kept me through it all.

SHARIFA

I AM
An Overcomer

Many of you, like myself, have faced unforeseen circumstances in life. Coming from a toxic family of instability and aggressiveness, my childhood was met with many instances of bullying, domestic violence, and not having a voice. However, over time, I learned I no longer had to live in darkness; I no longer had to be afraid of people anymore, and I no longer had to keep quiet. Ephesians 5:8 tells us in the past we were full of darkness, but now we are full of light in the Lord. Through this verse the Lord opened my eyes to see how standing up for myself, no longer being a victim, but a victor; and regaining control of my life makes me an Overcomer. Now, I have the honor of sharing my story and showing up as an answer, a beacon of light to help others get through and overcome similar situations.

Growing up I always liked going outside to play and talk to other kids. My friends would call me the life of the party when I came around. Little did they know that I silently suffered from fear as a result of being surrounded by negativity, confusion, conflicts, and even bullying. At school, I would get bullied because of my stuttering and southern accent. In a childlike way, the kids would laugh and say, "You so dumb, you can't even read,"

OR, "You so skinny you look like a toothpick". I felt lonely and sad inside because if I told someone, I figured things were going to get worse. My sister was the only one who would come rescue me when she saw what was going on, so I called her my security guard.

I overcame being bullied when the Lord helped me to become brave enough to tell my teacher what was happening to me on the playground. As she watched out for me, at recess she would inform me to walk away and ignore them when they approached me. That technique made a big difference in my life as a kid. Sometimes keeping silent, walking away, and letting the Lord fight your battles is the most successful thing you could ever do, to avoid conflicts.

In 1995, at 18 years of age, now a high school senior living from house to house, I met someone who was two years older than me. I thought he was the best thing in the world that could ever happen to me at that time. He was very sweet and treated me nice. Oftentimes he'd surprise me with a trip to the movies, shopping, and going out to eat. On many occasions, we'd go out of town on the weekends. I felt like I was on cloud nine with goose bumps all over my body whenever in his presence. He was good looking, tall and charming – or so I thought – until I noticed there was a dark side to him.

Two years into our relationship, I began to notice a wide range of insecurities, which led him to be very physical and emotionally abusive to me. The first red flag revealed itself as I was getting ready to go out with some friends. He became very irritated and controlling, picking a fight and accusing me of cheating, although he was the cheater. During the altercation he threw me on the bed literally breaking my fingernails, slamming my head up against a cabinet door, hitting me in my face and busting my lip. I felt so ashamed and embarrassed when others would see me out because of the bruises. Yet, like many others, I would make up excuses that I ran into the wall or slipped and fell. He would apologize by saying, "I will never hurt you again," and surprise me with a pair of shoes. **I stayed because I didn't know any other way around it, didn't have a place to call home**

He was so controlling that I feared looking out the window while riding down the street. He would make me look straight forward, fearing I'd want another man. During this time in the 90's, we were using pagers instead of cell phones. He would page every twenty minutes if I wasn't at work with a 911 code. If I didn't call back soon enough it would be hell when I got home.

After another confrontational incident in 1997 with a woman he'd been seeing, I found myself feeling rejected and isolated in a sunken place of darkness, searching for a way out. Ironically, it was in this darkness where I found the strength to leave, saying, "No More!" After praying, I heard the Lord say, "Go back to church, the place you were before you met him; I will help you". When I started to trust Him again, my life began to change for the better. He started sending angels my way who provided me with my first car and my own furnished apartment.

Almost two years later after marrying my husband of 19 years, I found myself in yet another compromised situation that would last for 17 years. This time it was with a church that offered very little to my spiritual growth. I lacked understanding of the calling on my life. I kept feeling in my spirit that I was an encourager with an assignment to teach young people. But when I excitedly shared this with our leadership and church members, I was hit with a bullied religious response, "You must be saved first." Well, in my eyes I was already saved. Their response made me feel so low, unworthy and underestimated all at the same time, which caused my faith to be shaken. Now, I found myself questioning God about my existence.

As time went on, I became discouraged and stagnant in my spiritual growth. I stopped caring about uplifting others or even wanting to put a smile on other people's faces. I remember saying to myself, 'I thought being a child of God was better than this; it has to be.' All I wanted was to understand what and how to use my gifts. So why did I stay so long?

I stayed out of the need to please other people, fear of more rejection, and fear of stepping out on faith. I didn't want to hurt anyone's feelings due to the fact that our small congregation was family. Although, I was informing my husband I wanted to leave due to the lack of spiritual growth, he rejected my cry, insisted that we stay, and that it would get better. I held on out of obligation to my husband as the head of the family. At one point, I did think things were getting better when an opportunity arose to coordinate a summer bash. Unfortunately, I hit the same wall of excuses. The 'straw that broke the camel's back', came when inquiring about needed supplies and simply wanting more information to coordinate the event. When sternly told, "YOU KNOW THE PROTOCOL," I was taken by surprise and felt bullied. To my knowledge we did not have a specific protocol to talk to the pastor about certain things. Standing there feeling total rejection, again, I said, "No more!" I no longer cared about leaving the congregation, family behind to seek my God given destiny.

As women, I encourage you to pay close attention to the red flags and the vibes you feel when something doesn't seem right. Red flags are indicators to warn us of something going wrong in our relationships. Be careful who you allow yourself to get close to and ask yourself the following questions, 'Do I fear him?' 'How does he treat his mom, sister or even himself?' 'Does he go to church, love the Lord, and does he really love and respect me as a woman?' When you find yourself in abusive situations, be reminded of God's Word in 1 John 4:18 that says, "Where God's love is, there is no fear, because God's perfect love takes away fear." (International Children's Bible)

As for your spiritual growth, you must do what's best for you. Be willing to come out of your comfort zone in order to see what all the Lord has for you, even if it means leaving family and friends behind. It's not always easy, but I do know the Lord wants you to try, even when you feel insecure. God tells us, "No, in all these things we are more than conquerors through Him who loved us" (Romans 8:37,

NIV). Let your confidence be lifted and your voice be heard in the name of Jesus! Know that you are coming out and you're coming out stronger than ever before. Let your light shine!

By the grace of God, You are Strong! You are Beautiful! You are Loved!

You are An Overcomer!

I AM

Favored

Enough

Evolving

Fearless

Restored

Chosen

Found

Resilient

An Overcomer

I am who GOD says I AM.

My *Reflections*

I AM _____

I AM WHO GOD SAYS I AM

LIVING MY LIFE ON PURPOSE

KIESHA

I Am

Who God Says

I Am!

I AM WHO GOD SAYS I AM

When you mention "The Bricks" to many New Jersians, they know exactly where you are talking about. That is where I was born and raised, in Newark, New Jersey, as the youngest of four girls, to the parents of Gloria Peterson and Thomas Peterson. Or so I thought. It wouldn't be until I was twelve years old that I would learn my real father's name was Earl Williams and I had three younger sisters.

As a child, I didn't know the call God had over my life, but I did believe in God. I was raised in the Pentecostal church. We went to church every Sunday, no matter where we lived. We moved between Newark and Vauxhall, a small town smack-dab in the middle of Union, Springfield, Maplewood and Millburn.

I lost my mother at the age of fifteen during one of the most important times in a young lady's life. While preparing to celebrate my Sweet Sixteenth Birthday, God saw fit to call my mother home. Instead of celebrating my birthday on the day of my birth, we were celebrating the life and times of my mother. After my mother passed away, I went to live with my sister and her family in Union, New Jersey. Since I had lived there before, it was easy to get reacquainted with my old friends and make new ones. My friends were happy to see me, yet they wondered how I could manage to still smile, laugh and be happy. I had to explain to them that I reminded myself of the good times my mother and I had. I did not focus on the many times she was sick or in the hospital or that I could not go to see her because I was not old enough to visit. While growing up, my mother taught me that we should rejoice when someone passes away and cry at the birth of a new baby. At first it was confusing, but she explained to me that when someone passes from natural causes, they are no longer sick and in pain. They have received the ultimate healing. However, when a child is born, we mourn the things a child may have to endure in a society where RIGHT is WRONG and WRONG is RIGHT thinking is an accepted norm.

As I got older, I carried what my mother taught me, but I still had to make some mistakes of my own in order to learn my own lessons.

I became a Clerk Typist for an insurance company at the age of nineteen. I was spreading my self-sufficient wings and had my own apartment and car. In my position, I worked in the Auto Department and was responsible for typing the insurance policies that were sent out to the insured customers. Eventually I started another Clerk Typist position in the Workmen's Compensation Department. My duties included drafting checks for Workmen's Compensation claims once the adjusters approved the payments. Payments went to claimants and doctors.

On January 26, 1991, I gave birth to my son, Earl Isaiah Davis.

On February 14, 1993, I married my oldest daughter's father.

On July 27, 1993, I gave birth to my oldest daughter.

So, roughly within two and a half years, I had two children by two different fathers. What I didn't have at this point was any idea as to what God had planned for my life. By society's standards, I felt like I was definitely going in the wrong direction. I do not remember how the idea came about to send checks to my husband if the claimant had the same name. I followed our scheme and we got away with it for a while. Then one day, I was called into a meeting. That was the day I was fired from my first and only job. After that day, I promised myself I would never do anything illegal like that again. I also promised myself that I would never get fired from another job.

I was sentenced to probation since it was my first offense. My husband was sentenced to six-months because of his prior history. I lived with my stepdad in Irvington, New Jersey. However, my probation was in New Brunswick, New Jersey and without transportation, I was unable to check in as needed. I never knew I could have had my reporting location transferred to the county where I lived.

With two young children in tow and I and my husband out of work, we eventually lost our apartment and temporarily moved in with my husband's aunt in Newark, New Jersey. I was able to get public assistance and Medicaid. I was also able to sign up for a program called M.O.E.T. - Mayor's Office of Employment and Training. The program paid for me to go to school and I was given a stipend at the end of each week. I attended the Essex County College Training Inc. Program and studied AutoCAD (Automated Computer Aid

Design). Funny how after graduation, I never did obtain a position as a CAD Technician.

A few months later, I was hired at the East Orange YMCA as the Receptionist. My husband and I had just moved into a new apartment with our two children. Even though we were on Somerset Street in the heart of Newark, I liked the area. I was just around the corner from my dad and one of my aunts. It was in close walking distance to transportation and the neighborhood pharmacy.

I remember the day of my arrest like it was yesterday. It was a nice warm summer day in August. I had on a cute sundress with matching sandals and a little purse. I carried a jacket because the air conditioner in the Y was always on and it always functioned very well. I saw two people come in, one a Caucasian man and the other, an African American woman. Both were dressed in suits, so I knew it was business. As my duties required, I greeted them, "Welcome to the East Orange YMCA, how may I help you"? They replied, "We're looking for Kiesha Peterson". In an instant, my heart sank to the bottom of my feet. I knew exactly who they were and what was about to happen. I replied, "I am Kiesha Peterson". From the YMCA to Essex County Jail, to Middlesex County Jail is where I spent the next fifteen months away from my family and friends.

That truly was an experience. Here I was – this church girl, choir member, usher - incarcerated for the very first time in my life. I was at the Middlesex County Correctional Facility in New Brunswick, New Jersey for fifteen months. I was accepted to a program for first offenders called ISP - Intensive Supervision Program. This program is considered to be more stringent than parole, but because of the life I lived, the rules were no problem for me and easy to follow.

One of the stipulations of the program was to find gainful employment, and that I did. In spite of my background, I became a Teacher's Assistant for the Essex County College Training Inc. Program. Through them, not only did I become an Office Assistant (Intern) for 10,000 Mentors mentoring program, that experience led to my becoming a full-time Clerk Typist for Rutgers College of Nursing. After that, I went on to become Administrative Assistant to former Assemblyman William D. Payne of the 29th Legislative District. From there, I obtained a position as a Customer Rep/Team Lead for H& J Ventures.

Many in our society (on both sides of the legal fence!) would have ex-offenders thinking that once they have been incarcerated, sustainable living wages is a thing of the past. In spite of what I had done in my past, I was still able to obtain all of those jobs. Why? I had made some lasting, notable impressions on some people before my troubled period in my past. Through it all, I maintained my trust in God, no matter how many times it felt like He was so, so far away. Without a doubt, He maintained my mind, my thoughts, and my actions. I admonish you to never throw in the towel and to never give up because giving up is truly NOT an option.

I implore you to make some lasting, positive impressions in others' lives. Pave some roads and paths that you may be glad to travel again one day. Never let your past dictate your future. No one is perfect. God knows all about us - the ups, downs, ins and outs. So, if you do decide one day to throw in the towel, you are entitled to throw it in, but ONLY to trade it for a clean one to carry as you pick up where you left off.

Second Timothy 1:7 tells us: *For God hath not given us the spirit of fear; but of power, and of love, and of a sound mind* (KJV). I encourage you to be the best version of *you* that you can be, because as I decided some years ago, *I Am Who God Says I Am*. And so are you!

Live Your Life on Purpose!

I AM

Favored

Enough

Evolving

Fearless

Restored

Chosen

Found

Resilient

An Overcomer

I am who GOD says I AM.

My Reflections

I AM _____

I AM WHO GOD SAYS I AM

LIVING MY LIFE ON PURPOSE

I AM WHO GOD SAYS I AM

ABOUT KIESHA L. PETERSON

Minister Kiesha L. Peterson was born in Newark, New Jersey to parents Gloria Peterson (Culver) and Earl Williams, and was raised in Newark and Vauxhall. She is the proud mother of three, E. Isaiah Davis (daughter-in-law, Cherelle A.), Ahja D. Smith and Toby S. Peterson and an even prouder grandmother of five.

Kiesha's ministry journey began on November 29, 2015 when she gave her initial sermon at her home church for over 40 years, St. Paul's Calvary United Church of God, under the leadership of Bishop Claude L. Campbell. She is the founder of *The Absolute Word Ministries* and has served as the Founding Host of the internet radio program, *The Gospel Hour Show*. Her love for writing emerged at the age of thirteen. Today, she is an Amazon Best-Selling and International Best-Selling Author, contributing as a Co-Author to *Stories from The Pink Pulpit: Women in Ministry Speak!*, *She Shall Rise: Empowerment for Kingdom Women,* and *The Pieces of My Platform*.

Kiesha is also a Self-Publishing Coach and Self-Published Author. Her solo work includes *7 Roadblocks to Success and The 3D Steps to Knock Them Down*, *Knowing When Enough is Enough: My guide to building your self-esteem, Book of Poems, Vol. 1* and *I Am Who God Says I Am*, under the pen-name G. C. Peterson. She is currently working on her fifth book *Be the Best You-You Can Be*. Her work has also appeared in *Women's Frontline Magazine* (November 2017 - cover story and April 2019) and *Victorious, Virtuous and Valued Magazine* (January/February 2017 issue 19).

In addition to ministry, writing and coaching, Kiesha is a Motivational and INpowerment™ Speaker and a proud member of The Soul Restoration Center, The Pink Pulpit, NAACP Tri-City Branch (Silver Life), National Council of Negro Women, and Women's Speaker Association

Kiesha served as Administrative Assistant to former Assemblyman William D. Payne, 29th Legislative District. She earned her Associate's Degree in Criminal Justice from Everest University (Tampa).

Minister Peterson's desire is to continue to walk the path that God has laid before her.

OUR SUPPORTERS THANK YOU!

THE #FIRSTSUPPORTERS MENTIONS

DIRECTORY

Pamela Adams
Discovering Life's Possibilities
www.discoveringlifespossibilities.com

Anterica Baylark

Amber Broadway

Clarence Brown, Jr.
CBJ Landscaping
clarencebrownjr4747@gmail. com

Kanisha Buchanan

Angelina M. Camacho

Church of the New Covenant | Pastor:

Apostle Jeffrey B. Kearney

Mother Helen Clyburn

Vanessa Collins | Vanessa Collins LLC

Sabrina Davis | Just Be Natural

| jussbnatural@gmail.com

Colby Easter | LimeLife Beauty Guide

Barbara Edwards

Beverly Fooks

Inesha Housey | Nesha's Sweet Treats | Nesha37@icloud.com | (973)204-2277 (Text)

Kafi Hunter

Rita Hunter

Waleed Hunter

Termesha Jackson

Mother Lois Jennings

Apostle Brenda C. J. Johnson

Yolanda Johnson

Sharon Jones | QueenDominion Enterprises, LLC

Kenneth Keys

Walter J. Lewit Drugs

Felicia Lucas | His Glory Creations Publishing LLC
felicialucas.com

Lakell Maxwell

Erica McBride

Maria Mosley

Mashunda Oliver

Jennifer Pitre

Cheryl Polote-Williamson, Founder

| Soul Reborn Victory Center |

www.soulreborn.org

Charles N. Price

Maureen Randolph

Riconna Reddix

Aundrea Rogers

   Minister & Mentor for Women

Saint Paul's Calvary U.C.O.G. | Pastor:

Bishop Claude L. Campbell

Patricia M. Seams

Dr. Onika L. Shirley | ASV's Global Mission Initiatives

Denise M. Shufford

Crystal Siclait

Candace Smith

Tamara Sneed

Kia Stewart

Ikepo Talabi

Jessica M. Taylor

Sheri Timmons, Owner | Grace Shared, LLC |www.GraceShared.com

Nikkia Troublefield

Vickie Dortch

Pastor Wilma Scott Warren, Founder | Regeneration Courage to Change, Inc

LIVING MY LIFE ON PURPOSE

Darius Watson | LAW Photography

| www.LAWPhotographynj.com

Pam Wiley | GP's Chocolates |
Treats for All Occasions | (908)875-8417

BOOKINGS, TRAINING AND CLASSES FOR KIESHA PETERSON

E-mail
MinKieshaLPeterson@gmail.com

Phone
(973)814-4814

Facebook
MinKieshaLPeterson

Twitter/IG/Periscope:
MinKLPeterson

Website:
www.KieshaLPeterson.net

IN MEMORIAM

To My Mom & Dad

Gloria Peterson

(8/1/1937 – 9/22/1985)

Earl Williams

(6/21/1946 - 9/22/2016)

I miss you both, there's not a day that goes by that I don't think about you. I hope and pray that I am making you proud.

IN MEMORIAM

To My Aunt
Christine Reed

(10/25/1935 – 7/11/2015)

What I wouldn't give to come over to your house to laugh and talk about life, and to just hear you say, "Things will get better."

The Visionary

MINISTER
KIESHA L PETERSON

CAROL CRAVEN

DEANA WILLIAMS

DEBRA DAVIS

LIVING MY LIFE ON PURPOSE

JENNIFER
NSENKYIRE

JUANITA
GAYNOR

KOCYSHA
LASHAUN

MICHELLE
FLAGG

MONTELL
MCCLAIN

SHARIFA
STIRGUS

www.thescatterbrainedgenius.com/publishing

www.ingramcontent.com/pod-product-compliance
Lightning Source LLC
Chambersburg PA
CBHW060527100426
42743CB00009B/1452